KALEIDOSCOPE

Cat Russell

To my mother, Beatrice, who has always been there for me.

Table of Contents

Life and Death Side by Side

"Backyard"

In this Spring
languishing under Winter's
unrelenting grip, the green grass

clashes with barren brown trees,
bare of leaf except the
few small buds peaking out
on the farthest branches.

Birds sing subdued songs,
as though afraid the snow will hear
and come again, shivering them
out of their seasonal homes.

Meanwhile, sprouting dandelions
rebuke the dead leaves laying on
the green grass: weed and seed,
life and death, side by side

just outside my window.

"Cheapskate Mid Life Crisis"

Motorcycles are too much:
speeding down highways
costs in broken limbs already
prone to osteo, too much money
from a bank account already
paying for meds and doctor visits
and replacement heating pads
that burst in the microwave
from overuse.

Give me a simple can of
spray-on haircolor...youthful hues
will coat my fading vanity
in rainbows of blues and pinks,
greens and even silver--
not old woman silver
that shines with passing years
but the strangely bright I like
to think belongs to Tolkien elves
but closely mirrors
cheap bagged Halloween wigs,
those plastic and polyester strands
gleam as brightly
as the halos of tarnished angels

"Losing the Thread"

my hand's grip too fragile,
the threads pull just beyond my reach,
lighter than air,
I watch them float away

they look so beautiful
growing smaller with distance
like birds sailing on solar winds
darkening the sky with their shadows

Kaleidoscope: poems by Cat Russell

"My First White Hair"

I found my first spot of white
last night
           on my chin

on my goddamn chin

then dreamt of Mother Nature,
forever young
her cascading grass
green ringlets in disarray,
alongside Father Time,
his aged hoarfrosted face
crinkled with years and fears,
as both cower cornered against the ropes
in eternity's boxing ring.

They beg me for mercy
with pleading eyes and moist cheeks,
fingers splayed before their faces,
awaiting wrath made real.
How dare they age me before I'm old.

My hands become my grandmother's
   gnarled arthritic claws
   that caused me to see the future
   in orbs of crystal,
      showed me how to pray, to say
   each strand of rosary,
   to read the leaves of tea
as I deliver blow after blow after blow

as I deliver blow after blow after blow
   they grasp my mother's walker,
   the transportable seat she's forced

to use to support those legs she used
to dance with my father every weekend.
The aluminum cools my palms
as I bash it against those grass green curls,
knock out Time's gleaming white incisors.

My arms transform, polka dotted with age,
to my father's mother's strong long limbs
that taught me to roll gingerbread
dough, baked my birthday cakes with
brightly lit candles that blew out but
always came back for more. I pull them back
to smack the bloody grin from Time's grinning skull
again and again and again. Screw him.

In my mind's eye, I grasp the walker of my mother
with the gnarled claws of one grandmother
and the sagging spotted arms of another,
deliver blow after blow with the walker and without,
right hooks, left jabs, gut punches
like the ones those two have given me.

Aging before my time?
I won't go down
without a fight.

But when my reverie breaks,
I smile, take
my tweezers,
and pluck that sucker out.

"Mourning Dandelions"

In my front yard, the dawn brings out
golden lions lounging in emerald grass.
Their teeth drip sunlight. Perhaps later,
I will harvest those bright blossoms
for an herbal infusion, light and sweet,
to celebrate May's arrival.

I hear the lawnmower's low growl.
Those sharp lion teeth can't survive
the sharper blades cutting, splitting,
ripping them from the ground until

they come back again bright and beautiful.
Nothing keeps them down for long.

"First Fib"

My
heart
beats with
the rhythm
of lightning striking
each cloud's spotless silver-lining.

"scar tissue"

my heart ripped clean
still beating from my chest
replaced with something new
pale toughened tissue
where a heart used to be
less vibrant less yielding

still beating

"Grieving"

Miserable and wretched
The sun does not warm me
When I go to kiss your lips
The turn of your cheek burns

My stomach churns
The shards of my heart
Slice through muscle and bone
Internal bleeding pales my tongue
I feel so alone

I want to atone for my unknown
Skin shivers from your absent touch
Your face swims before my eyes
Your expression blank

What did I didn't do?
What can I?
Your silence rips me apart:
the question I dare not ask.

Before sleep I debate
not saying I love you
so I don't have to hear
 you not say it back

"3a.m. Elegy for Peace of Mind"

Gone with misfiled papers
Gone with weekends no longer my own
Gone with facing my fears
and taking a chance on failing
--at which I succeed
as my veins throb
my eyes ache fingers
toes stretch pop crack
teeth tighten jaws fasten
in place all I want right now
right now is sleep sweet sleep
instead I lay here aching sheets
smelling of nothing but cold
heartache as a thousand
demons and ghouls make nests
in my chest of future plans
obligations what can I do
what should I do should I
have done that I didn't couldn't
falling short my steps hurried
careless no matter how careful
I trod my own feet trip me
I'm going down how
how do I pick myself up
when I can't even sleep
can't even breathe
for the goblin
sitting on my chest
stealing the air from my lungs

Kaleidoscope: poems by Cat Russell

"Blue"

I know that tomorrow I will be alright
I'll look up and be sunny again, but

today

right now

the weight of the sky presses me down.
I'm drowning in its blue.

"My Worst Enemy"

knows my weaknesses
breathes into each ear
my deepest doubts and worries

preaches cowardice
disguised as caution,
tells me to wait on others
instead of my own instinct,
hushes me when I should speak,
barks at me to scream when I should quiet,
inflames me when I should calm,
hesitates me when I should
shake off her icy grip
and leap into unknown waters,
toes extended, arms wide, swim
against the current
til I reach the place where I create
my own sun-dappled shore.

"Traitor"

This morning I awoke to the news
our world leader may be a traitor
a sexually harassed girl was burned alive
a disturbed man brought gasoline
and lighters into Saint Patrick's cathedral
a rock icon committed suicide
a local poet died

yet this smile is traitor
to this world I inhabit,
because I smell the warm toast buttering the air
and hear my son's videogame downstairs
and all I can think is

I'm still breathing.

"Doppelganger"
  for Angela

She walked by me
wearing your countenance
along with a grey shirt
and matching pants,
a little thinner,
a little older,
her brown hair bobbed
round a heart shaped face
so close to yours
I'd swear she was your ghost,
then she was gone,
I left wondering

Remembering the last time
I was here, you were
still alive.

I open the door to exit
the welcome center washroom,
surprised to see her
on the other side
as though you'd come back
to tell me it'd all been a mistake,
        you were alive and well,
but all that really happened
was I held the door open
rooted to the spot, and

she passed me by.

"Borrowed Robes"

When my father died,
his thin cotton robe was
the only thing I took

The maroon fabric
kept his scent, the cologne
he wore every day

Each time I wear it,
I feel his arms around me,
keeping me warm.

Often I borrow
my husband's castaways,
big enough to swim in

When he's away, I sleep
in his shirts, too long
to wear anywhere else

Each time I wear one,
I'm enclosed by loving arms,
his balmy embrace.

Who will wear my clothes
when I am gone?

Kaleidoscope: poems by Cat Russell

"The Gift"

Li Po's poetic heir explains why
he destroys his poem after reading:

gifts are only given once, and I imagine
those torn papers floating downstream
or sacrificial flames engulfing verse,
rising smoke lyrics for the gods to enjoy.

Why can't poems be given more than once?
Each reading--a sown garden of rock and sand:
the hard elements remain but with wind
and days the pattern will change.

I've reread my favorite verses many times.
What would I give to hear them read anew
by creators long dead and gone? Yet their words
live beyond the short years of their lives.

As lovely as that gesture is, I want
to gather those torn pages, mend them
with strong fast silver threads. I want
to press them between my palms
like the bright petals of plucked dandelions.

I long to keep what's given.
Poems may be lost to time
but a single reading is not enough,
not for me.   Not for me.

Words, like breath, are too precious.
They change the world
with each exhale.

Kaleidoscope: poems by Cat Russell

*inspired by the poet Sony Ton-Aime reading at
Latitudes Poetry Night, Akron, Ohio (Sept 2019).

"Becoming Versed"

thoughts in dark recesses
sorted arranged ordered becoming
in the safe spaces between these lines

transforming unmarked crisp sheets,
stained with each crimson effort,
becoming raw emotions captured

like ink dripped into a well
becoming sweet aromatic passion
poured into forms profound yet silent

"Poetries"

the marrow in these bones,
red ink flowing
through these veins,

breath in these lungs,
each divine exhalation
expelled into the world

the words on this page,
crisp as autumn leaves
caught by errant winds,

or ideas like balloons
that rise above the clouds,
soar through fields of blue

Kaleidoscope: poems by Cat Russell

"Performance Poetry"

not dead words on a page
lifeless stale flat
letters strung together
like the lights of a holiday tree

but crowded lonely loudly rhythmic songs
breathing change into the wider world
breaking beats swaying tongues
dancing to the groove
vocalizing new thoughts
whispering ancient truths

"Embroidery is a Poem"

Choose just the right threads
Complements against contrasts
Stark enough to stand out
Bright enough to shine
Dark enough to draw in
Shape each piece tight
enough to hold but not break
these thin delicate strands
Carefully cut what doesn't work
Replace with what does

Fill the spaces between
Uniting the whole

"A Prayer for Poets"
"Aren't poems the same as prayers?"
-- Jill Bialosky, Poetry Will Save Your Life

May we write
hymns of homonyms,
linguistic litanies
celebrating ambiguities
lingual, cerebral,
emotional, and chimerical.
We worship words
for both meaning and texture,
invoking Merriam,
not forgetting Webster.

Please, hear our pleas
for definitions that defy
concision and clarities.
Give us doubt, obscurities,
double-entendres, uncertainties:
fertile soil, abundant means
in which to plant our fevered dreams.

Devoting ourselves daily, we
adore imagery, metaphor, simile,
meter, and musicality.
We vary our lines of Freeverse,
compose haikus, sonnets, Fibonaccis,
rhymed or not, searching for the sublime

with our every word,
we pray.

"Profane"

a stream of profanity
oozes from my lips like air forced from tires
pressed against hot steaming asphalt,
like water spreading slowly, a puddle growing
in dark dirt, in fast lanes overflowing
from deep cracks spilling from each pothole
slickening roads with danger and damage,
oils and filth reflecting rainbows
against city arteries, cars sliding farther
than they are meant to go

the real consequences often
unintended.

"F bombs"

What the hell is this profanity?
the lazy-man or -woman's crutch
when they can't find the right words
words shocking enough
to blow your mind, your brain
right out of your head
grey matter splattered upon
the wall you beat your head against.

Why fall back on a single word
as verb, adjective, noun, adverb
with just a little tweaking,
a holy hell bobcat on acid fix
infix fixing our lingo til it rings
true to intent. Our fan-freaking-tastic
psychotic psychedelic expression of
anger, pain, joy, angst, ecstasy.

Why swear by the same word
so frequently? As if it's on standby
waiting to be used, a paratrooper
ready to step into nothingness,
the wind roaring,
then silent,
then the peace
before his fall disguised as landing
lands on solid ground, knocks air from lungs
becomes speechless. Why call on

the ever ready F-bomb ready
to be dropped with deadly accuracy?
Why not swear with visceral alacrity?
By Thor's sweaty balls
calls more to mind

than sex's crude synonym.
By the orange skin of our 45
inspires more terror.
By Janet Jackson's pierced nipple
shocks more than simply saying the same word
over and over and over again,
as if shock value increased with familiarity.

With enough vehemence any combo
can pierce eardrums, let off angry steam
threaten to boil the brains of heated vocalists.
But the F-bomb has become
so common, so basic, so familiar
that profane connoisseurs reach for it
for all occasions: the foundational F,
the one size fits all
blaspheming little black dress.

Familiarity breeds not just contempt
but laziness too, the lingual fallback
when creativity fails, when brain juice
runs dry, drained like wells we run to
driven by thirst or thrift.

Every word has a perfect use,

but if you think
an F bomb should be used
for every little thing, think again.
Whether they're nouns
or end in -ing, I drop them with care,
because despite their versatility,
though they can be shocking
or mundane, boring or funny,
they do not fit every context.
The little black dress

sometimes strains at the seams,
no matter how we accessorize.

Fuck THAT.

"Word Magic"

thoughts made solid on each page
lift ink-stained swirls
reaching the gods, themselves
inkling thoughts made flesh,

so sympathize, empathize
with the words themselves,
those fetal deities do not die,
for who could kill them?

Ideas are immortal.

"The State of Literacy in America"

This morning, my back ached,
my eyes strained,
and my fingers cramped
with the constant clicking
and typing I performed,
saving free eBooks
of poetry to pillage
throughout the coming year.

I checked my local library online
for events in my area,
returned and downloaded new content
from its digital collection,
perused graphic novels lining
online shelves
for me to access 24/7.

In the past year
I've read
few paperbacks and hardcovers.
Instead, I've consumed eBooks
and digital comics checked out
at a moment's notice,
downloaded Shakespeare,
listened to more music
than I have in decades.

The masses
weep for the state
of literacy in America,
the decline in reading books,
the slow erosion
of bookstores in cities
and the changing face

of the nation's libraries.
If printed pulp alone
counts as literature,
my literacy has declined
in the past ten years.

I am a bibliophile without books.
The stories and ideas and histories,
inspirations and facts float
about my brain
via electronic ether.

Hollow Roots of Fire

Kaleidoscope: poems by Cat Russell

"Kaleidoscope"

Today I wondered
what a group of butterflies is called.
I'd heard them called a storm,
imagined them thundering through the sky
on gossamer wings, sailing on solar winds,
circling through the atmosphere
perfuming the air on paper thin wings

Today I looked up
what a group of butterflies is called.
Some call them a rabble, but
I can not wrap my head around
this term applied to such beauty.
I see them in my mind's eye
flying in perfect sync, disregarding
reality, no common insects but
metamorphic miracles,
rebirth realized on feather light wings
bright with the colors of the rainbow

Today I researched
what a group of butterflies is called.
They are sometimes called a swarm,
but that term is forever wedded in my brain
with bees buzzing round hives, slaving
over honey, hovering over fragrant blooms,
stinging small boys who run with overflowing eyes
for mother kisses to heal their hurts;
not the almost silent flight of delicates
like colorful wrappings
tossed aside after their gifts are opened
floating upon a summer's breeze

Today I discovered

what a group of butterflies is called.
Their name is Kaleidoscope,
a term that makes perfect sense,
their colors swirling together,
blending with the seasons,
the ever changing pattern
a perfect fusion of shifting compliments:
the envy of artists, flowers, and clear blue skies.

"Pandoring to Beauty"

For every Pandora or Eve
releasing evils into the world
there's a sleeping Beauty waiting
to be rescued.

For every Devil
tempting mankind to damnation,
there is Prometheus
sacrificing heaven to save mankind from darkness.

The tree of knowledge
blazes with Divine fire,
both burns and benefits
those who dare to use it.

There is nothing good nor bad
but thinking makes it so.

"Cassandra"

I feel like when I warn
the worst is yet to come,
I'm overlooked, never heard
but always right.

If I changed my name
to Cassandra
and moved to Greece,
I might be understood

if not believed.

"Morpheus"

How I long for your touch
soft as smooth sheets enveloping me
in dreams of faraway lands,
your smiles warm me
like thick, cotton blankets,
your quilted embrace
shields me from the cold.

With voice sweet as nightingales
you sing me to sleep.
Embraced, seduced by your lullaby,
I never wish to wake.

Heaviness pulls me beneath,
weighs my eyes with the day's cares.
Your eyes gleam silver moonlight.
Waves of silken hair fall across my pillow.

The darkness outside summons me
to your arms. We run together
in fields bright with poppies and lavender,
otherworldly worlds filled by creatures
of myth and magic.

"Achilles, the Heel"

Greatest of Greek warriors that fought
upon the soil surrounding distant Troy,
you fought with the strength of a demigod,
yet you are most (in)famous for
                              your weakest part.

"Nuclear Shadow: Hiroshima 1945"

a contradiction in terms
a permanent darkness
burned by bleaching all
except people
becoming atoms
becoming nothing
their bonds dissolved
by unbearable light
embracing the darkness
forever

Kaleidoscope: poems by Cat Russell

"Notre Dame Burns"

Quasimodo's perch
A new spire of flame
for all the world to see
smokey fingers reach
for heavenly intervention
from an absent god

Her cathedral lights up
the evening cityscape
its burnished curves glow
orange against the Parisian night
backlights songs
of mourning and hope

the city holds its breath
the world holds its breath
a smoke eater fights
for breath
while the world watches the fire die

The news covers all
the city, the nation, the world
sighs that this monument
this masterpiece, this historic treasure
is saved

The worst has been avoided,
we're told

Of the smoke eater there is nothing.
no questions
no answers
no watching eyes

Isn't a human life
as newsworthy as a burning building?

"Easy Bake Insides"

absent windbreaks
kindling landscapes
a dragon's heat caught
inside a tree's dying heart
crimson scales burning
hollow roots of fire
its white ash wake

"Operation Babylift"

Flight plan from Agent Orange
and unfriendly fire, the war torn
to new homes stateside
its first flight
airlifting from Vietnam
the orphaned ones
their parents lost too soon
too soon
too soon to see them grow up
instead strapped in carriers
on airplane seats,
the innocent ones witness
not new homes in a new land
but fuselage
breaking
burning
the rice paddy skid
the soft meets hard
flesh and metal and pliant plant life burning
burning
burning
the dam breaking
drowning waters and unfurling flames
the damn breaking apart
the smoking metal skeleton
the smoking
the
the fragile lives lost
their legacy
their memory
their deaths
fading
                    fading
fading

lost to time
who remembers the orphans now?

"1,362 feet"

Holding hands
Falling faster than thought
The rushing air takes their breath away

inspired by victims of 911 who fell from the Twin Towers

"Ode to Marie Curie"

Chernobyl on the Seine
Barbed wire walls and surveillance
cameras can't dim   the desire
to see inside your lab, to take
a radiant piece of history,
radiating for years to come.

Arcueil still glows from the fame
of your infamous discovery:
labcoats brimming with those
incandescent blue-green vials,
such fatal beauty brought
about your own pallor, the key
to treating the Twentieth Century plague:
killing carcinoma swifter than its victims

So many years later, but not
long enough, policemen and thieves
expose themselves to particles
poisoning their blood, blackening
the plants outside your lab
shelves filled with double-edged swords
cutting through the next thousand years
if we are lucky

Cancer patients could thank you for their diagnoses
wonder if your headstone glows as brightly
as the particles that won your fame,
martyred you on the altar of knowledge

Both you and your notebooks rest in lead-lined boxes,
deadly treasures

Kaleidoscope: poems by Cat Russell

***inspired by** <u>Chernobyl On The Seine: Marie Curie's Lab</u> <u>Is Still Full Of Nuclear Waste</u> - *Technology* *(culturacolectiva.com)*

"Cavaliers' Parade"

Cavaliers' parade
Championship
not for just the team
but the city of Cleveland
city streets shut down
jam packed with fans
I've traveled far
paid for parking
walked for seeming miles
to see
celebrity and celebrate.

Yet I still can't see
through the throng of bodies
lining the street, I spot my perch.
I climb a nearby tree,
Sun shines brightly bathing the crowd,
but leafy branches spare me its glare.
The building is *so close*.
No stairs, but lined instead
by flat clear windows.
Its third story lacks balconies.

I lean or leap, shimmy up concrete,
my feet propped between two columns
supporting my weight in lieu of floor.
Mindless of those below   or above

All I know is I have the perfect view
as I gaze
--not at the crowd swelling beneath
not at those beneath my feet
Not at fame within arms' reach--
but at my phone's viewscreen.

This is how I choose to participate
--hovering between life and death--
in this perfect moment.

"Disney Parade"

Pinocchio's a puppet again.
Ariel's regained her fin.
The handsome Prince regressed
to the beast he's always been.

Their storybook endings fictions
pandering to those unseen multitudes
but never change who they are.
We never know another's unknown life,

only the parts they choose to share.
We rarely choose   to truly see.

"Onion Heart"

Peeling back the layers
to get at what's beneath
inside bittersweet
with bite
*inspired by comments of Ohio Beat Poet Laureate John
Burroughs*

"Robin Wright"

I love that I live in a world
where Princess Buttercup grew up
not to be Princess
but an Amazon warrior

I love that I live in this world
where princesses rescue
the ones they love
as well as themselves

*Robin Wright is the actress that starred as Buttercup in The
Princess Bride and later as Antiope in Wonder Woman.*

"Servings"

He buries his face
in the flowing folds
of her long hair,
inhales her scent
like a man sniffs the air
above a Thanksgiving turkey.

She is his meal,
each morsel of her
served up for his consumption,
digested, discarded as easily
once his appetite
is sated.

He picks her clean
then leaves her lean,
empty and exposed.

***inspired by a scene from Hulu's Original Series: The
Handmaid's Tale.**

"Inner Light"

i hold myself together
with mind thought matter
what matters is the light
the light inside shining through
the cracks of consciousness
my bruises darkly immaterial
my skin paled but tender firm
my eyes closed but open
to the inspiration inside
listening to that little voice
knowing i'm never alone

i'm everything all in one
majestic maternal
blindingly brilliant
my light outshines
my body's darkness

the breaks aren't flaws
the breaks are the reason
i shine so brightly

inspired by tweet via @me_brady *at 8:09pm on December 29, 2019:*
https://twitter.com/me_brady/status/1211454350343593984

"Steinism"

I dreamt
I visited Gertrude Stein's apartment
in Paris
and viewed the paintings
but not herself.
I stayed in the "other" room
and spoke with Alice
because
I was a "wife,"
and that's the way she did things.

If I had been myself,
I don't think I would have

though the temptation
to view an early Picasso or Matisse
fresh paint barely dry
might have weakened my resolve.

In Paris the poor writer comforts himself
with the knowledge that the paintings
always look better when he's hungry.
Why should his wife starve
from more than one type of hunger?

Did their host keep the paintings
in the room with her and her male guests
or spread throughout the rooms...
for even the "wives" to enjoy?

Maybe I would have looked first,
then spoke later

for the sake of the art.

inspired by Ernest Hemingway's A Moveable Feast.

"Skeletal Remains"

In visions of the dark night
I have dreamed of joy departed—
But a waking dream of life and light
  Hath left me broken-hearted.

The sighing wind
gives breath to the darkness,
the stars lighting the ebony sky
like pinpricks of God's grace
that pierce the blackened heavens
with dazzling white.
Who would dare disturb this quiet,
wake those that haunt deserted paths?
The North Star, our pilot light, guides us
In visions of the dark night.

My eyelids close, lids lowered against
the terrors that make me tremble
and seek solace beneath warm cotton covers,
my shield. The witching hour strikes--
a time too late for the faint-hearted
that quake and shake and turn away
from what they--what we
--cannot bear to face: the lonely dead,
quiet and disregarded.
I have dreamed of joy departed—

What dreams may come to those
that can not face their fears?
Sheltering beneath shut lids
holds no solace for those whose terrors
follow them beyond the veil
of sleep: the blight
of a million cares and worries,

the looming spectre of loneliness
a demon--no longer out of sight
But a waking dream of life and light.

The daytime hours filled by
the demons that haunt my nightly dreams.
I look within myself each dusk
--trapped between the sun's escape
and the rising moon,-- unguarded
yet I find imprisoned courage.
When shall I be released?
This time--too long before
I meet my dear departed--
Hath left me broken-hearted.

> **glosa of "A Dream" by Edgar Allan Poe, written for the*
> *Day 9 prompt of ReadWritePoetry courtesy of Cuyahoga*
> *Library, in honor of National Poetry Month.*

"Suicide Note"

Those who choose death
by oven, shoving their heads
deep into the darkness,
speak their final act,
this is my life, served up
for your consumption,
dried up insides
stuffed with nothing
but what others wanted,
nothing left
of myself,
for myself...

The gas, without
sight or smell,
kills them, or
maybe it's ignition
like Buddhist monks
that burn themselves
in public squares,
protest by immolation,
a statement in fire:
nothing is permanent,
everything changes
and moves and
lives and dies like
these flames consuming us...

"Falling Fruit"

perhaps it was
that same apple that fell
on Eve's head
and got her
into so much trouble

that fell on Newton
and jogged his thoughts
not of Godhood, but
of the Heavens

of celestial bodies
turning in the void
expelled from
their own garden
nursery, birthplace
of stars
and humanity

Thank heaven
for falling fruit

Kaleidoscope: poems by Cat Russell

"Inertia"

The tendency to stay at rest
or to stay in motion
mortal enemy or best friend,
stagnating year after year,
growing older, never moving
against the current, across the tide,
leaning into the wind or riding
the crest of the wave

Newtonian physics
in the social realm,
Laws of motion do not change,

but people, even those stagnating
in the rest that eventually becomes eternal
can move themselves
            with just the smallest push...

"Vision"

Minds measured
not by genius
but girth,
projecting away
from this limited
sphere, density
into higher dimensions,
hyper-thick
towards inspiration.

"Entropy"

Feelings once so strong and violent
fade to the background
of daily life

Become the quiet hum
of existence

"Curvature"

I long to reach out
in the direction space curves,
stretch beyond my limitations,
see what surrounds me
hidden from view

To float above this, spying
not just inner space,
but over, under and through,
Not pierce the veil but shred it,
Not float above but soar, fly
in directions unknown,

See with my eyes
things only imagined.

"Tomcat Physics"

The wave function collapses,
sets free Schrodinger's cat
to pester Peter at golden
gates of inlaid pearl   or,
brane thrumming, roam
streets filled with exultation
to feast on rats lush with
blood and fat juicy flesh.

His quantum paw prints
pitter patter through
Reality, ana jumps
and kata falls through
spaces we can't see;
he's a confused jumble
appearing, vanishing,
growing, then shrinking
to nothingness in the
something beyond
our sight.

Unknown M space
his tomcat territory,
out of bag and box,
he won't be held back,
a wild scat cat
ratatat-tatting 'cross
space and time,
howls of pleasure
rebounding off gravity's
smooth curves.

*inspired by Rudy Rucker's book, The Fourth Dimension:
Toward a Geometry of Higher Reality*

Kaleidoscope: poems by Cat Russell

"Starstruck"

You expect an explosion to make noise:
a vibrant blast, the roar of a thousand tiny particles
zooming outward from a single point,
a boisterous, destructive, mind-blowing cacophony
of delirious dissolution of something so big
our brains boggle at the thought of its scale,
only vaguely comprehended when wrapped round
inane imaginings of the smaller things
we experience in our everyday,

except we know sound does not travel in a vacuum.

Yet the stars themselves are heard
as static on radio telescopes, background noise
in a universe so vast that the nothing between
its rainbow-hued nebulas,
its solar systems filled with spinning planets,
asteroids circling each burning sun,
and comets wandering through galaxies
bursting with wonders yet to be known
cancels all out to zero:
space itself the ether molded by gravity's waves
surfed across by light in the cosmic ocean.. .

We know sound does not travel in a vacuum.

Why then, when a star supernovas,
are we not deafened by its silence?

"The Uncertainty Principle"

You can never know the position
of another's heart
with any precision unless you know
their velocity of mind,
the course of their thoughts
relative to you.

Knowledge requires facts.
You can never know
what another will do over the course
of years or minutes or the seconds
it takes to wipe away tears of joy
or regret. You can never know
everything they think, they thought,
why they did not act, why they did

where they choose to live
and breathe away from you,
what they feel when the wind is icy
but the sun warms their skin,
how exactly they experience you
when you are gone.

Knowledge requires facts.
You can never know
the position of another's heart.

All you can ever do is believe.
That's all that is required.

Halos of Tarnished Angels

Kaleidoscope: poems by Cat Russell

"Atheist ThanksGiving"

I'm thankful for my family and friends,
food and shelter and all the other things
I can't imagine living without.

I'm thankful for poetry and words,
books and breath and cinnamon rolls
toasting in a warm oven spicing the air.
I'm thankful for premade meals
I can reheat and claim as my own,
a working heater in a world of snow,
warm puppies and cats, and
a machine that washes my clothes
so I don't have to, electricity
powering my home, for hot tea
in cracked china cups, steaming kettles,
and cookies to dip, brightly colored embroidery,
and YouTube videos telling me how
to stitch each technicolor thread,
for artists, textured paintings,
sculptures of fabric and wire,
mobiles of origami birds soaring
through indoor air, and metal chimes
tuned by each passing breeze.

I am thankful

to this boundless mass
from which all I love has come,
the first atoms burning inside the stars
etching our signatures across time and space,

making all this love I feel possible.

"Gentle Reminder"

You are an activist, and so am I.

Every choice we make is an act, a
vote for good or ill--Life is not neutral.

The only ones on this earth who are not
activists with every word and deed

are those who no longer breathe.

"On Hearing of The War"

What war?

The war that's raged
almost as long
as my son has lived
the war in the Far East
the war in Iraq won weeks,
or was it a month after the invasion?
The war to secure our safety
thousands of miles away.
the war that some died
but not many
in those first days,
no the casualties piled up
they pile up
reported slowly at first
roadside bombs
and other mishaps
incidental
to secure the peace

bodies brought low
then brought home
flags draped like tired curtains
covering cold flesh costs
hidden from our eyes
our consciousness
our consciences

as news trickles
to almost nothing
news of those few dying
year after year after year

when is a war not a war?
we go about our days
unaffected by those losses
unless they become personal
unless they are
our sons
our daughters
our fathers
our mothers

no victory gardens
for almost two decades
of ongoing war
won in a few weeks
years ago
yet going on

no celebrations
of victory
no remembrance
of sacrifices made
families destroyed
orphaned children
body counts

our only acknowledgement,
should they become visible,

Thank you for your service.

Kaleidoscope: poems by Cat Russell

"Radius"

The radius of our supposed safety shrinks
with each new news report,
from north African atrocities
to mass shootings in our schools,
the schools like a high school in Florida
not so far from where I grew up, from
where I lived with my infant son and I think
Thank God we moved from Florida,
Thank God we moved to Ohio
to a better place for a safer and
quiet and peaceful life, then the news
blows away that notion of our
quiet and peaceful hometown schools,
schools like the one in the next school district
where a seventh grader was bussed before
he blew himself away in its bathroom, shattering the
quiet and peaceful murmur of muttering students
in its halls and classrooms, the quiet and peaceful
schools of Ohio--and my first thought was
Thank God he didn't hurt anyone else--
surrounded by libraries and learning
and nearby parks and woods, woods
where two teens were found blown away,
murder-suicide or suicide pact--no one knows,
--and my first thought was WHO?, my second,
Thank God they only hurt themselves,
quickly followed by a search to discover their identities
--a fruitless search that yielded other details
details besides names: the two went to my son's school,
one in my son's graduating class,
and it happened in the quiet and peaceful
field behind his friend's house, the field
where we looked at animals through his friend's
sliding glass door, no way to know

but word is it was one of their neighbors
just sixteen years old and a seventeen year old boy.
What were they thinking? and
what else was blown away? How fragile
the circle of our safety is, how blown away
with the pull of a trigger, with the thoughts
our thoughts, our minds blown away by
each nearer tragedy, each closer closing madness,
and ALL I can think is
THEY WENT TO MY SON'S SCHOOL
and
THEY WENT TO MY SON'S SCHOOL
THANK GOD THEY DIDN'T MURDER ANYONE ELSE
THANK GOD THEY DIDN'T KILL MY SON
because the radius of our supposed safety keeps shrinking
the circle of rope round our collective necks tightens
and we're running out of air

Kaleidoscope: poems by Cat Russell

"Clean Slate?"

once the day's scratched
across its surface
no matter how you rub
a trace always remains

you cannot rewrite your past
only print the present
over what came before

"Choose"

When we have radios
When we have television
When we have libraries
When we have free public computer access
When we have free wifi
When we have free podcasts
When most Americans have smartphones
When injustices are frequently caught on smartphones
When those videos are free to see online
When social media links to legitimate news sources

When it takes a matter of minutes to inform yourself
to find out both sides of an issue
to verify the truth of reported facts
to research and form an informed opinion

When we have near limitless access to information
Ignorance is a choice.

"Every Little Thing"

I'm just buying shoes
(probably made in Chinese slave labor camps)

or eating lunch
(of slaughtered animals)

or having dessert
(made with cocoa harvested by child slaves)...

I didn't know.
I didn't want to know.

I work hard. I just want to be left alone.
Don't I deserve to live my life without
getting hit over the head for every little thing?

Who was it that said,
"Life's about the little things..."

Oh, shut up. I'm a responsible person.
I'm a responsible person.

I pay my bills, my taxes, donate to charity.
I'm responsible.

So I'm not responsible for the way the world is.
It's everyone else

but me.

"Active"

Nothing comes from nothing.
     So do
     SOMETHING,

and do it from love.

"A Woman's Place"

A woman's place is
in the home
in the kitchen
in the nursery
in the Resistance
in the Senate
in the Capitol
in the White House
in the workplace
in the boardroom
behind her man
behind her children
behind her family
behind her cause
behind herself
in any goddamn place she pleases

filling the room
with her goals, her love,
her dreams, her ambitions,
her abilities, her wit,
her wiles, her presence,
herself
because a woman can do
what she wants
because a woman can be
who she wants
because a woman answers
to herself

That is the only imperative

"Death"

We spend our days dying
each moment transmuted
to something new
Twilight colors fade to black
the better to sleep, rest, repose
with eyes closed and the day's rose
grasped tightly in thin cold hands

Dawn cannot come without night
The sun must set before it rises

Kaleidoscope: poems by Cat Russell

"Elevator"

Four closed close walls and a door
transport cargo to each passing floor,
a trap to the woman who shares this tin prison
with a single male occupant   she doesn't know

Something so innocuous to one
A danger to the other
a smile on her face
as she grips her keys with clenched fist

just in case

"False Hope"

Such a thing's not possible.

A hope is just a wish, which can not be untrue.
The desire lives on, the longing for beauty,
the dreamer may wake, lay one shining brick at a time, build
golden castles in the air.

Don't hold on to false hope, the practical will say
As if lead never becomes gold, picked flowers
never speak in poetry, stars never wink, or the moon
never rains silver in the dead of night.

Naysayers be damned. Live on hope.
It matters not if the goal is reached,
as long as you keep reaching.

Kaleidoscope: poems by Cat Russell

"Buddha Day"

I have never celebrated Buddha Day.
Until this afternoon, its existence
never occurred to me.
We celebrate the birth of Christ,
a person I believe lived a powerful life
if not as divinity incarnate,

so why not the legend of Siddharta?
          celebrate the birth of a babe,
one who took seven steps,
pointed both up and down,
and declared his own importance
to the world?

I don't understand.

Buddhism teaches its followers
to recognize absence of self, our egos
like drops of water thinking themselves
separate from the ocean they are part of.
Why then did baby Buddha declare,
I alone am the World-Honored One?

I could fill the ocean with
the things I don't understand.
Buddha experienced enlightenment
like color, something seen
rather than taught.
Does ignorance equal bliss,
when a cup must be empty
before it can be filled?

But, today, as my thoughts swirl
as Brownian motion

in a freshly filled china cup,
to pour tea over an image of the baby Buddha
seems oddly poetic and peaceful.
The ritual, I'm sure, is sweet,
and I love the taste of tea.

"Candles"

I light candles for those lost.

Over the minutes, hours, days
of my short lifetime, will they
become as infinite as candles
ignited on a cake lit
for the ageless universe?

"Crucifix"

Natural poetry in the transformation:
an instrument of torture and death
becomes a symbol of peace,
the translation transcending both.

Medieval monks used crucifixes:
a knife blade hidden within the wood
of one, another sharpened to a point,
shape lending itself to function.

Knights swore on swords as crosses:
metal points sunk deep into the earth,
converting instruments of violence
into divinity of form.

--the yin and the yang,
back and forth over and over,
the loss of equilibrium
makes it hard to see the way.

"Crossed"

poetry of peace
from torture and death
crossed edges make
their metaphorical point
sharpen bloody protection
from evil more solid than divine
used by knights to send foes
to premature afterlives
before using the same blade
to pray for their victims' souls

"Spiritual Matter"

If Spirit is the immortal
part of ourselves,
the essence of our being,
Matter is Spirit.

Where else would our essence lie
but in our deepest parts?
Deeper than the cells of our skin
that flake off with touch and time,
becoming dust breathed by the world.

Deeper than the muscles beneath
that shrink and grow with age and years,
the smooth use that pumps them large,
the slow stretches, the proteins building
the ability to push and pull
and leap and bound and even lie down
when life becomes too much.

Deeper than the cells making up
each separate part, each particle,
each electron, each quark
of up, down, strange, charm, bottom,
and top--their varied homogeneity
unites us with all. The dung beetle with
it's beautiful shimmering body,
the dullest bird gracing the heavens,
the plastic bag floating discarded
in far-reaching oceans, each
unappreciated dandelion gracing
a freshly mown lawn with sunlight-
yellow petals, until it rides the wind
as cotton seedlings--visceral swan song
embodying the paradox

of uncreated creation.

We all come from each other.
Atoms are celestial: our
common building blocks
compose infinite variety,
We are made of star stuff.

Materialism is Spiritual.

We share each other's lives.
We breathe in each other's essence.
There is nothing deeper
than realizing how our impermanence
permanently imprints us
on each other.

"No thanks"

Gifts require nothing
from those who receive them,
not even a widened smile
of unexpected joy

"Ahimsa"

Harsh words buy harsher deeds
in a world in dire needs of gentleness
not just to our fellow man but woman,
child, ant, earth, and foaming sea

Breath on kindness spent's a better deal
for all that breathe our common air, share
this common blue. No action's wasted:
each grain of sand becomes a mountain

with time. Avoid violence dynamically,
not just with votes we cast but meals we eat,
each step we take with bare feet, aware
of our weight, our toes curled in naked earth

Don't just vote a better candidate,
but consume a more peaceful palate, walk
as though each blade of grass has voice,
each spider is a Charlotte

Every choice we make matters,
No choice we make is small, all
create this world we live in
so choose harmlessness with care
intentionally

"Foretaste"

The smell of oncoming storms
fills me with expectation,
the jack in the box
just before it springs,
the joke in my pocket
a punchline waiting for its moment,
the birthday present
an instant before it's opened

The taste of anticipation
salivates my tongue, readies me
for each exquisite moment

"Library of the Damned"

You and your delightful spear would pierce your sides
bleed beauty on each page and rejoice with the rest of the
damned in another addition to their unbounded
unhindered collection.

"Heaven and Hell"

Heaven and Hell exist
inside the heart and mind you carry within you

everywhere you go, ecstasy flows within
your chest holding a devil's dark conscience

God does not choose where
you choose to dwell

"Pain"

We know we are alive
not by the agony of loneliness
but the basic aches and pains of existence,

know by the way they sharpen focus
on the simple pleasures of each moment.
That's something

the dead miss.

Kaleidoscope: poems by Cat Russell

"Things I'll Do in Hell"
 --reaction poem to Chris Martin's "Things to Do in Hell"

I'll create with artists, troublemakers, rule breakers:
        splatter paint alongside Pollock, shape
        jubilees with jet engines, lace words, converse
        with Coleridge, write lines with Whitman
        --intersperse free verse with limericks,
        stitch rebellion
                        into existential tapestries.

I'll tune in to the music of the spheres:
        spin ellipses like CDs burning through the heavens,
        consume heretical symphonies, croon Blues with
        every wistful soul, savor each melody sung,
        alleviate heartaches, gyrate with
        the rocks n' rolls of the lates and greats,
                        pound rhythms relentless as heartbeats.

I'll party with those who know how:
        dancing on sunbeams,
         drinking like Hemingway,
                bathing in champagne,
                        loving with abandon.

I'll read every banned book ever written,
feet propped on a stack of freshly burned paperbacks,
while away the eons
        by the rosy glow of eternal flames.

All the interesting people,
All those prohibited pleasures,
All the time in the worlds
                await me there.

Hand me that forbidden fruit.
I ache for something juicy.

"Apocalyptic Piggybank"

Saved for a rainy day, the rainiest,
the Noah and the Flood's nothing compared
to the shitstorm plunging from the skies day
night afternoon twilight dawning new day
of the dead, of the dying, of the neverending
circle of life, death, then whatever comes next
before it begins again, a new currency
for the new day, bartering beans and rice
and crowbars and weapons, anything's
a weapon in the end of days, even a clay
piggybank filled with nothing of use, just
the remnants of a dead civilization
preserved as tarnished copper coins
graced by long-gone Presidents
no one will remember.

Kaleidoscope: poems by Cat Russell

"Don't Bury Me"
> --reaction poem to "Three Things" by Jim Hanlen (Rattle, Fall 2017)

The earth can't hold me.
My eyes give sunsets to the blind,
My lungs give breath to the breathless,
The marrow in my bones gives strength
gained through past days
so another may endure

My spare parts flame away, dust carried
by warm southern winds through azure skies,
floating alongside cotton pink clouds...

"Cakeism"

I've never understood
the phrase "have one's cake
and eat it too", as if
cake were a thing to have
and not eat, making it part of you
until, on less savory terms,
it's parted from you

Do I want to have my cake
and eat it too? Of course, but maybe
it's not an admonition of restraint,
a warning I can't have it all, so much
as the realization of one simple reality:
everything degrades in time.

"flesh"

the grocery store is giving itself a facelift
moving the makeup aisle directly across
from the butcher counter
the place where flesh is sold
I wonder on the idea of consumption
how appropriate this is

The reason strip clubs have buffets

"I. Hate. Bullies."

I hate the way they lay in wait
at the bicycle rack,
knowing you can't go home
without that pit-stop,
they talk to and about you
while you fumble, unlock,
pull the plastic-wrapped chain
through wheels and metal frame
to free your bike   to be free
of those circling round you.

I hate the way I didn't stand up
for myself, took verbal punches
because boys didn't really hurt girls,
only beat them down with words
cut deeper than knives, invisible
wounds could translate to self-inflicted,
but why risk damnation to avoid
the torment of people I loathed?

I hate the way I don't
have a time machine to tell
my former self to stand up,
not let time slip by,
stop being afraid,
to learn to take chances
while they can be.
Years fly by;
the cliche holds true:

My biggest regrets: the things I never did.

"Predator"

Once as a young girl
I walked home from school
alongside major roads
cutting through fields
walking past the same
cookie cutter homes
with neat yards mown
caged by metal mesh
containing sometimes good
sometimes friendly small dogs.

Once as a young girl
I'd shoulder my backpack
packed heavy with textbooks,
back aching with their weight
and wonder who lived within
those flat painted walls
as I walked the last few blocks home
avoiding strangers because
of all the milk carton kids
I'd heard about on the news.

Once as a young girl
on a steaming sidewalk
a stranger in a car
called to me for directions
I yelled them to him while
I struggled with my bags
remembering all the tales
of kidnapped kids who talked
to strangers in strange cars.

Once as a young girl
that stranger's car followed me

slowly down the street
when I refused to come near.
I remember my cold fear,
the creeping whisper of its wheels
turning, turning, turning
against the asphalt
for seconds, minutes, I don't know--
it felt like hours until

Once as a young girl
I walked to another home
I hoped did not have a dog,
unlatched their metal gate,
entered their backyard,
cut through to the next,
hiding along the way,
watching to make sure
the car did not see me
or where I went so
he would not find my home.

Once as a young girl
I walked to my own home,
used my key to enter
alone   as always,
made myself a shake,
and watched *ThunderCats*
before I started my homework,
all the while wondering
if he followed me home,
feeling foolish because
it was probably nothing
nothing
but my imagination.

Once a young girl

was followed by a stranger
who asked for directions
in the twilight hours
when she was alone.
She walked away, then ran
with the awkward gait
of someone who knows she's alone,
knows no one will help her
if she screams.

Once a strange man
asked a young girl for directions,
then asked for her name
in the twilight hours
when she was alone.
He followed her as she walked,
then ran, relishing the way she fled
like a newborn fawn,
the way she turned to make sure
the predator was not close
enough to pounce.

Once a strange man
relished that fear, fed on it,
enjoyed her focus,
how important he felt to her
as she ran for her life.
Blind to the contradiction,
he savored her fear,
found joy in her terror,
all the while claiming
he meant her no harm.
Her fear was enough.
Her fear his harmless fun.

As though assaulting her peace

of mind was no crime,
as though someone who preys
on the fears of the young
will never ask for more,
will never do more.
He called it harmless.
He called it fun.

He suggested others try it.

Some people will do anything
to leave their mark on this world,
even if all they leave
is a stain.

"Alphas"

Worship of a god replaced by
Worship of the state

We're programmed for reverence
always looking to the alpha

the one above the ultimate
Lord Buddha mowed down

Chairman Mao raised up
How exactly is religion

the only opiate of the masses?

"Don't Mind Me"

He says he doesn't mind
non believers joining the group
to protect our children
in our public schools,
as if religion were
prerequisite
for parental love.

The curriculum is clear:
conform or be cast out.
The answers are known,
The answer is always known.

I believe believers miss the point.

Paying no mind,
they don't mind me.

"Final Moments"
--"My life flashed before my eyes, only I wasn't in it."--Ray McNiece

What will I see before I close my eyes forever?

I am the watcher, not the watched.
The observer, not the actor
in my own play, but a player
observed by those who may recall
my acts with their own final breaths.

Hope I get a good review.

ACKNOWLEDGEMENTS

There is simply no way to thank all the people who have helped me reach this point in my writing journey, but I especially want to thank Sandra Feen for extensive feedback on this manuscript, as well as her unwavering generosity and support. She is quite simply one of the kindest and most talented people I know, which is more meaningful given the fact I know so many.

I would also like to thank John Burroughs for taking the time to review this manuscript and contribute a blurb, for founding *Crisis Chronicles Press* which has produced so many incredible books of poetry, and for kindly publishing my first book, *Soul Picked Clean*.

Thanks also to Doc Janning for his kindness in reading this manuscript and consenting to a blurb, for his dedication to the promotion of the craft, for his beautiful words, his inspiration, and for creating events for poets to ply their craft in these difficult times.

I am deeply grateful to William F. DeVault of *Venetian Spider Press* for giving me the chance to work with him once again by publishing this collection. His efforts and extreme patience are very much appreciated.

I'm also indebted to the northeast Ohio poetry community, Massillon Public Library, *Literary Cleveland*, *Latitudes Poetry Night* (Akron), Cleveland Library, Cuyahoga County Library, and *The Write Stuff Writers' Group of Canton, Ohio*, all of whom have either inspired or given feedback on words within this book.

And, as always, last but not least, I want to thank my family for putting up with me throughout the years, for enduring odd schedules and long talks, for working to support me in my endeavors, for inspiring me, challenging me, listening to me, for being my rock and wellspring. I love you all.

CREDITS

Originally published on *52250-A Year of Flash* (Sept 2010, credited as Catherine Russell): Every little thing

Previously appeared on my writing blog (Cat Russell | Writer, Reader, Bibliophile Extraordinaire (wordpress.com)):
Skeletal Remains (April 2017)
Spiritual Matter (Jan 2019)
Traitor (May 2019)
Operation Babylift (Sept 2019)
The Gift (Nov 2019)
Clean Slate? (Nov 2019)
Achilles, the Heel (Dec 2019)

Previously appeared on my Patreon as a Poem Dissection post (www.patreon.com/authorcatrussell):
--Operation Babylift (Sept 2019)

My Writing Niche 2.0 **(podcast** July 2020)
--Cheapskate Mid Life Crisis

Thirteen Myna Birds **(Summer flock/July 2020 via *BloodPudding Press)* –**"F bombs" and "Cheapskate Mid Life Crisis"

About the author

Cat Russell shares her life with her high school sweetheart, their son, and another ferocious creature in the wilds of Ohio while writing stories, composing poetry, and learning more about the craft every day. Her work has been published in print and online, and she is the author of three books: *Soul Picked Clean* (March 2019), *An Optimist's Journal of the End of Days and Other Stories* (August 2020), and *Pinholes: Traveling through the Curtain of the Night* (November 2021).

She publishes monthly via her writing blog (www.catrussellwriter.wordpress.com) and Patreon (www.patreon.com/authorcatrussell), as well as maintains an online social presence via FaceBook (@ganymeder), Twitter (@PoetCatRussell), and Instagram (authorcatrussell).

Kaleidoscope: poems by Cat Russell

Kaleidoscope: poems by Cat Russell

Lightning Source UK Ltd.
Milton Keynes UK
UKHW021936031022
409877UK00003B/133